Other Works by the Author:

Plays

Rock Paper Scissors
Planting Firewood
Upright Position
A Box of Yellow Stars
I Bet They're Asleep All Over America
Neither Honey Nor Vinegar
Bob War
Pack Up the Moon
Earlybirds

householes

a collection of poems inspired by
the female voices of Veteran Caregivers

poems by

Natalie Parker-Lawrence

Finishing Line Press
Georgetown, Kentucky

householes

a collection of poems inspired by
the female voices of Veteran Caregivers

Copyright © 2024 by Natalie Parker-Lawrence
ISBN 979-8-88838-480-0 First Edition
All rights reserved under International and Pan-American Copyright Conventions. No part of this book may be reproduced in any manner whatsoever without written permission from the publisher, except in the case of brief quotations embodied in critical articles and reviews.

ACKNOWLEDGMENTS

"householes," "marine's daughter," and "no one teaches girls," were first published in *Unlikely Stories*, October 19, 2022.

Publisher: Leah Huete de Maines
Editor: Christen Kincaid
Cover Art: Gloria C. White & Associates, Memphis, TN
Author Photo: Julia A. Finnell
Cover Design: Gloria C. White & Associates, Memphis, TN

Order online: www.finishinglinepress.com
also available on amazon.com

Author inquiries and mail orders:
Finishing Line Press
PO Box 1626
Georgetown, Kentucky 40324
USA

Contents

PTSD

households not foxholes	1
marine's young daughter	2
no braces for me	3
arizona ranch	4
adopted nephew	5
pest control in maine	6
where you goin now?	7
rude government employee	8
sister and my man	9
suicide watches	10
explosion in the back seat	11
by hook or by crook	12
family conflictions	13
need a new plan, not now	14
mother says I walk too slow	15
grieving in the shade	16
waiting since april last year	17
he left me for another	18
soldiers with no families	19
base housing, then now	20
color blindness	21
conure diablo	22
california fire	23
family fight in san juan	24
every homemaker wants these:	25
from icu	26
ten minutes: shop and hide it	27
friend asks you, doin okay?	28
not into kids? we got five	29
street food in puerto rico	30
restrepo, afghanistan	31
no foraging game	32
with a heavy wrench	33
where are you going?	34
you would think hospitals know	35
i can move away, but i	36

save the younger kids 37
a hard night's day plan 38
sick tired and crazy 39
goal ultimatum 40
you can't scream at me 41
if body duty 42
you know how some people is 43
looking for a good normal 44
without a window 45
do not rearrange or buy 46
i didn't have it 47
no one can see me 48
ny state of mind 49
sitting outside in the yard 50
either or neither 51
not getting thirty dollars 52
decided to stay 53
i hope you die soon 54
spider webs down there 55
memorial day 56
mama always says 57
can't get plane to guam 58
the vet will the red trailer 59
spider babies are called slings 60

DEMENTIA

mowing not mowing 63
this new gal is cute 64
pick up your laundry 65
he waits at the door, ... 66
often in silence 67
deer (not) standing up 68
i bought a new boat today 69
short-term breakfast memory 70
why we can't go out 71
brand new hearing aids 72
i love the grits there 73
aim for direction: 74
hallucinations 75
when your husband's sick 76

you told my husband	77
this, every morning	78
this morning he swore,	79
things ain't been goin too good:	80
since i'm a christian	81
crazy parrot squawk	82
get dressed, get blessed, try…	83
i said i didn't	84
frozen all inside	85
a month ago you told him	86
he forgets my name	87
i seed the driveway	88
call uber, not a limousine	89
he put cat litter	90
why did he let them keep them!	91
i just stand and watch	92
putting in my teeth	93
they're inside the walls	94
seeking shed antlers in the snow	95
when you see your dad	96
going out to eat	97
I get in my car	98
selling the mattress	99
some girlfriends, not all	100
no one teaches girls	101
september 6 dream	102

Human life itself may be almost pure chaos, but the work of the artist is to take these handfuls of confusion and disparate things, things that seem to be irreconcilable, and put them together in a frame to give them some kind of shape and meaning.

—Katherine Anne Porter

The idea is to write it so that people hear it and it slides through the brain and goes straight to the heart.

—Maya Angelou

Dedications

To my parents, my parents, Robert Vernon Neely, Navy Veteran, and my mother, Dorothy Gallina Neely, his Caregiver for the last four years of his life. They always said to try new things even when they were afraid I would.

To my aunt, Martha Gallina Waldron and my uncle, Cmdr. James Edward Waldron, Navy Veteran, who were among the first in our family to try new things.

To Mrs. Ellen Marr, my fifth-grade teacher at Holy Rosary School, who told me I was a poet. When teachers tell you good things about yourself, believe them. When they tell you bad things, ignore them.

To my former students who are the children and grandchildren of Veterans, who are military Veterans, and who presently serve in the active military, I am thankful for your faithful service and resilience under duress, making homes wherever you and your families are transferred to and from.

To my husband and the love of my life, Cayce Lawrence, my nemesis in sixth grade, who believes in my work and me every day.

Introduction

In the United States of America, exists an army of brave and resilient Veteran Caregivers needing help, rest, and resources.

Their loved ones are Veterans who suffer from one or more chronic diseases, conditions, and illnesses: dementia, PTSD, ALS, MS, SCI/D (Spinal Cord Injury/Disorder, TBI (traumatic brain injury), Parkinson's Disease, cancer, mental illness, diabetes, hearing loss, skin conditions, heart, lung, and kidney dysfunctions, depression, and amputations.

Veterans, from the United States, Guam, and Puerto Rico, served stateside and overseas on military posts and bases, and in combat zones, in World War II, the Korean conflict, the Vietnam War, Desert Storm, the Gulf Wars, and Post 9/11 conflicts in Iraq and Afghanistan.

According to the Elizbeth Dole Foundation, 5.5 million Military Caregivers (over 90% of them women) take care of their loved ones at home. It's a formidable job for people from their twenties to their eighties, the majority, managing extreme events every day, can tell stories of dedication and pain, love and fatigue, patience and frustration, determination and isolation.

Every woman in these poems is a hero, and what they bring to the Caregiver experience is nothing short of extraordinary. Many quit their jobs to become full-time unpaid home health care workers. Some Caregivers are Veterans themselves. Most Caregivers, much of the time, forget to take care of themselves. Our job is to help them remember.

Most of poems here describe the ordeals of untrained women, yet devoted and diligent, Caregivers, who push through the front lines of offices and the phone lines of bureaucracies to request services for their loved ones. Some poems reveal the responsibilities of parents who have taken in sons and daughters. After having been wounded, abandoned, discharged, and divorced, some Veterans also bring back their own children to their childhood homes. Many Caregivers and their children suffer from and continue to suffer from domestic abuse, violence in the home, drug and alcohol abuse, racial prejudice, suicide attempts, and financial insecurities. Then the pandemic hit all of us with the tragic effects of the COVID-19 virus.

Because I wanted to protect the identity and privacy of Veteran caregivers, I used a hybrid haiku form: each line contains either five or seven syllables. No one can be exposed and compromised in counted syllables. At least that is my absolute intent. Two chapters, PTSD and Dementia, reveal the stories behind the two conditions Veteran Caregivers manage most of the time. As many Veterans get older, sometimes the Caregiver must contend with both.

These poems range from funny to bizarre to graphic to poignant to horrifying, written from my notes as a Training Specialist in the Caregiver Center at the Lt. Col. Weathers VA Medical Center in Memphis. I worked from home for two years during the COVID-19 pandemic, but, just like everyone, I contended with the illnesses and deaths of friends and family, disturbing politics, and natural disasters. To comfort myself, I collected the stories of forceful women. Together and apart we kept our houses together.

PTSD

householes not foxholes
    with or without him
        in the desert with mines
        spiders big as dinner plates
        no front lines, no blanks
    no peace here either

marine's young daughter
    asked for a princess phone, got
    a long cord instead
    anchored at her father's chair

no braces for me
        teeth pushed together
        by dad's rough fingers
        every night before bedtime
        saved so much money

arizona ranch
> seek the barn, save you.
> let him smolder on the porch.
> save the dog, horses
> from his cigarettes.

adopted nephew
        visits when we call.
        we bought his first high tops
        whispers, stop drinking

pest control in maine
    pick bugs off son's cat
    pound possums with sledge hammer
    pick bugs off son's skin
    pick off snipers, easier

where you goin now?
              out by tomorrow
              you want all my turnip greens
              you picture me with others?
              not the boss of me

rude government employee
    out with my son who
    quells my anger from his chair
    double amputee.

sister and my man
>	if she can't get you
>	she get you some kinda way
>	smile that smile? keep on.
>	beat you like you stole
>	something, lying dancing eyes.
>	hot grits on the stove

suicide watches
    pain hard to manage
    i need it to end
        i stole his bullets

explosion in the back seat
        hot car :::: canned biscuits
        hit my head. i saw my brains : :
                                        : :
                                     : :
                                                  : : heavy, white, doughy.

by hook or by crook
                i just quit last night!
       slurringgaspingslobbering
              methamphetamines

family conflictions
        to sister-in-law:
                you too ugly not to speak.
                my brother, my charge.
                you gave up the right.

need new plan, not now
> leave his sorry ass?
> when son graduates high school
> in about four years.
> that's when I can leave
> that's a long time to
> wait for a separate peace.

mother says I walk too slow
        her chair, upside down.
                get my cigarettes. you know
                i ain't got no legs!

grieving in the shade
    after her child died
    on a forest walk
    white fawn with pink eyes

waiting since april last year
        i bought a good wig
        when i got the stipend.
        damn alopecia

he left me for another
>	but now he's back home
>	suicide in the garage
>	rolled up the windows.
>	locked the doors, waiting,
>	with pills and whiskey.
>	the car, the motor running,
>>		just let him be gone
>>		shouldn't be too long

soldiers with no families
     these guys have no clue
     they worry about the world
     i teach them spanish

base housing, then now
> when she was little
> drank water at camp lejeune.
> twisted spinal cord.

color blindnesses
        cannot match his clothes
        can see past the camouflage
        can see spiders, snakes.

conure* diablo
    six inches tall green
    sleeps inside my son's armpit
    warm soft feathers

*small parrot

california fire
      why do I linger
      as my life burns to the ground?
      my heart, home, ashes

family fight in san juan
        he is exhaustant.
        acts like hot lion.
        i was so in chock.

every homemaker wants these:
        lemon pledge and playtex gloves!
        need a table first
        buy glass dishes next

from the icu
> his mother calling,
>> it wasn't the wreck.
>> it was that high blood pressure
>> that brung his coma.

ten minutes: shop and hide it
 you caint buy nothin.
  women get to feel pretty.
   i stole pink lipstick.

friend asks you, doin okay?
            yeah, i took one for the team.
            sex makes men calm down.
            i can take a breath.
            he took too many.

not into kids? we got five!
      you had an affair.
      you ended up living in
      your car. miss us yet?

    street food in puerto rico
          iguana tacos
                my husband eats them all up
                i no like kiss him.
                      me neither, girlfriend.

restrepo, afghanistan
    you talk of war, but
    don't see our daughter sobbing,
    in morning facetime phone call

    no-foraging game
           placed to compromise:
           beef jerky. if they grab it
           from under latrines
                    their sad hungry butts
                    kicked out of special forces,
                    must tell us wives why.

with a heavy wrench
        cracking the kneecaps
        of my sweet nephew
        gnawing green apples, dense noise
        like dark jungle leaves

where are you going?
    before leaving home,
        I scream into the dish towels ///
            separating us.

you would think hospitals know
        not to offer opioids
        to former addicts.
          he wadnt goin to say no

i can move away, but i
        don't have much to sell:
        no furniture, no good car,
        no appliances.

save the younger kids
        to get custody,
        use retirement money
        hire a slick lawyer

a hard night's day plan
        hair and fingernails
        don't grow, toenails bitten off.
        don't bite them off now.

sick tired and crazy
      from watching your kids
      brawl. i fight the urge to smash
      a mirror on them

goal ultimatum

        I told him last year:
        yer gonna take those new meds
        or get the hell out.

you can't scream at me
              you a sack of shit
    then say,
              hey give me a hug.
    it don't work like that.

if body duty
        is your only job,
        you can get messed up
        fishing up vietnamese
        floating near the boats
        lifting black coffins
        in san diego

you know how some people is
       work in big buildings
       they play volleyball on you.
       no matter what the
       size of the building.

looking for a good normal
        you cannot shove me
        against the blue bedroom wall
        while our son watches then hides

without a window
	had to quit my job.
	he stops breathing when i'm gone,
	prison: tan sofa

```
do not rearrange or buy
     stuff for a blind guy
       the new    sofa and                    the chair
       invisible       he
                              falls down cussing me
```

i didn't have it
>	she dint mean to hold
>	a knife to my jugular.
>	she needed her phone.

no one can see me
> driving with a flask
> between my thick thighs
> my two kids in the back seat
> ex-husband far gone

ny state of mind
       i love your southern accent.
             i just love your accent too.
     i have an accent?

sitting outside in the yard
    my wheelchair feels warm comfy
    inside, he's screaming.
    roses, thorny-red, but kind

either or neither
>	i'm gonna kill you
>	or you commit suicide
>	in your dirty barn.
>	just not in my clean kitchen

not getting thirty dollars
    i need some money
        for my scratch offs, beer, and weed.
            what about your food?
            i shake my head no.
        get me some tacos, woman!
            not no, but hell no.

decided to stay
      tarot cards don't lie.
      i sent the email:
      him, his lover, one hundred
      old friends, no secrets

i hope you die soon
> before the house is
> sold. then I can keep it and
> live here without you.

spider webs down there
      he lays a blue jean jacket
      on a bed pillow
      masturbates without
                               me

    memorial day
        one son was sent to iraq
            another son vanishes
            in california
            seven years later
            they find his body
            and the murderer
            in oklahoma.
take your husband to
cemetery to
relive vietnam?
pack a picnic lunch?
great furniture deals?
buy an appliance?

mama always said
    don't smile in pictures
    your face is crooked
        don't want to believe her.
        i practice in the mirror.
        in the mirror I practice
            amenenema

    can't get plane to guam
          colectomy, missing
          child with no eyelids
          hawaii not home
          paradise prison
          during COVID time

the vet with the red trailer
        digs a bigger hole
        for the horse, coco.
        positions his head
        toward the river
        says a sweet prayer
        brings our dog to say goodbye
        eagles, buzzards land too close

spider babies are called slings
    adult son lives with us
    keeps tarantulas
    locked in plastic apartments,
    one hundred in his bedroom.
    he breeds roaches for their food. N
    not crickets, he buys
    them at the bait shop.
    female spiders birth
    eight hundred to one thousand
    bring fifty dollars apiece.
    he names the spiders,
    buddha, nugget, jazz
    stinky, smoky, blue.
    blue is still alive
    stud of uneaten lovers

    husband is dying.
    husband wants to shoot my son
    does not want to die at home,
    because of the spider smell
    and they get loose some,
    but the hospital is worse.

DEMENTIA

mowing (not) mowing
        planted lawn mowers
        steel handles straight up
        croquet wickets for giants,
        arbors for dachshunds.

this new gal is cute
        breakfast oranges.
        he peels one for a stranger,
        used to be his wife.

pick up your laundry
>   *lord, grant me justice*
>   *against my adversary**
>   your damn nasty drawhs

*(Luke 18:1-3)

he waits at the door,
        (i'm in walmart, manicure)
watching people pass.
hurry up in there!
        loves it when i yell:
            kiss my big penis!

often in silence
        extremes magnify
                              that shit happened years ago
      i can't read your mind
                            she dint mean nothing
        then don't call out her damn name

deer (not) standing up
        if you're not first at
        deer season's opening day,
        you're last. believe it.

i bought a new boat today
                you sold it years back.
                              deep water, questions
                              continuous flow:
where's my new boat?

short-term breakfast memory
     bottomless coffee
     asks me for another cup
     the seventh with cream.

why we can't go out
      bowel accidents.
           drip through chair's steel spokes
           no real dignity in that

    brand new hearing aids
        FiRsT DaY WiTh RaInDrOpS
                EXPLOSIONS. ARMageDDoN
      uMbrelLla! INComin. . .

i loved the grits there
        the hospital grits
        brought by the hot nurse
        cheese grits. heavy cream.

        katrina blew down my house,
        drowned my recipes.

        at home, ten minutes.
        microwave your own damn grits.
        hot enough for ya?
        like broken concrete.

aim for direction:
        driving, the bathroom.
        men don't see things very well,
        whizzing by, on tile.

hallucinations
      he could see dead folks
      long time before dementia
      like a spirit guide.

when your husband's sick
        people don't call or
        visit anymore, do they?
        i'm the old new second wife.

you told my husband
        he don't have much time,
see his brown eyes. don't guess the
dead color later.

this, every morning
> i saw your worthless
> brother at the library.
>> he's been dead ten years.
> i know that!

this morning he swore,
> *never tasted it*
> every day of his life,
> he's eaten oatmeal.

things ain't been goin too good:
        foal died from colic
        but the black goat is pregnant.
        knees hurt somethin bad.

since i'm a christian,
        had to get over
        daddy molesting my son
        and my stepsister.

crazy parrot squawk
    daddy laugh at the same time
    comedy round here
    i'm about to lose my mind

get dressed, get blessed, try . . .
     every morning
     sometimes you need to scare him
     like a little kid:
     FIND YOUR SOCKS! PUT ON YOUR PANTS!

i said i didn't
> steal your teeth. neither
> did the new health-aide worker.
> the beagle neither

frozen all inside
        if you've been attacked
        for thirteen years by your dad,
        you got some real shit.

a month ago you told him
        thirty days to live!
        can't make a new appointment?
        today he stands!

he forgets my name
        blank eyes stare at me
        who even am i?
        except that white bitch
        handing him meds with
        too little water

i seed the driveway
    with shiny things: keys
   pennies, nickels, and quarters.
          mom grins, picks them up,
          gives them to me, her daughter.
          in her mind i'm an old man
               who throws them back down.

call uber, not a limousine
                i want to visit dora
(his mistress of twenty years)
i bring him the phone.
                she said no, don't come.
                now's not a good time.

he put cat litter
	on the red pansies
	as good fresh fertilizer
	god, help me swim the river,
	swerve the gray boulders

why did they let him keep them?
    embrace old metal
    wrath slides like chilled steel,
    guns, shiny swords, knives
    silver disobedience

i just stand and watch
>   nothing makes him glad
>   except playing with the dogs,
>   drooling on bunnies.

putting in my teeth
might help our call go faster.
 he can still do things.
 gather puzzle pieces? no.
 fold socks? not so much.
that was true before he fell.
 shop amazon? yes.

they're inside the walls
        family of skunks
        decided to move.
               i told you they was sneaky.
it's a damn nightmare.

seeking shed antlers in snow
      can't pull up his pants
      doesn't own a gun or knife
      looks for traces now

when you see your dad
        die in front of you,
         you don't want to see
         his cat put down at the vet.

going out to eat
        we don't do that anymore.
        after he chews steak
        sucking out the last juices,
        spits on the table

i get in my car
        and I drive away
        and crank up the sound
        sing with the music
        michael neil jimi
        ccr joni
        ronstadt marvin styx
        queen abba stones cream
        eagles santana
                if he needs me i'll be there
                but first, call the fire station.

selling the mattress
>	not using our bed
>	hospital sent another
>	a woman came to see it
>	smiled because she had never
>	seen a mattress that
>	wasn't used all up.

some girlfriends, not all
    stab you when they get a chance
    sutures come from cows or sheep
    not now, they're spitting
    stitches, weep plastic,
    trim the tails
                 of
                           knots

no one teaches girls
        to fall down with grace
                coaches yell, Slide and Get Up,
                Hey, You Aint Hurt Much,
                No Blood, Brush It Off.
        when he falls down now
        off the bed, wheelchair,
        i try to grab him
        i crash too, old knees.

september 6 dream
    ringo came to eat
    breakfast one morning
    and asked him to play the drums
    at the beatles' fall concert
            what should I call you?
            richard? rich? ringo?
                just call me *brother.*
    have they called about practice?
            waiting for him to get back.
    where you once belonged?

Gratitudes

Veterans for their service to the United States during war and peace times,

Veteran Caregivers for sharing their incredible stories during the COVID crisis,

Colleagues at the Caregiver Center at The Lt. Col. Luke Weathers, Jr. VA Medical Center,

My talented writing group: Bob Burns, Ron Gephart, Dawn LaFon, Steve Malin,

Friends who are essential and inspiring and not for just their artistic, writing, and editing skills: Evie Skoda, Karen Garrison, Ann Mary Mullane, Rebecca LeMoine, Marcia Aldrich, Sharon Griffin Farmer, Cheryl Whitehead, Margaret Edson, Chris Ciccarello, Patrice Melnick, Kay Murphy, Corey Mesler, Sonja Livingston, Virginia Bryan, Christine Lockhart, Donna Reed, Linda Johnson, Julia Finnell, Gloria White, Barbara Hatch, Liz Conway, Kristen Iversen, Jodi Jones, Virginia LaFon, Ariel Parker O'Brien, Celia Anthony,

The Low-Residency MFA Creative Writing Program at the University of New Orleans, 2008-2010, in Montpellier, France and San Miguel de Allende, Mexico,

Family members who are always ready to share stories, cook Italian food, and pour wine,

The Military Writers Society of America Writing Workshop, September 2019,

Members of the best Women's Book Club, still going strong after thirty years, for sharing food, wine, laughter, great literary discussions, and our lives,

The Caregivers who write and paint in the margins of their Bibles and their journals to get through the hard days and harder nights. Thanks for reminding me about the value of blank spaces,

Richard Wright, African-American writer, who, extremely ill in the last year of his life, produced over 5000 haiku poems, for being my guide: create art during chaos and tragedy.

Natalie Parker-Lawrence, teacher, writer, and editor, received her MA in Linguistics (Dialect and Literacy) from the University of Memphis and her MFA in Creative Writing (Creative Nonfiction/Playwriting) from the University of New Orleans. Now a Training Specialist in the Caregiver Center at the Lt. Col. Weathers VA Medical Center in Memphis, she was an instructor in the Communication department at the University of Memphis for eight years and taught AP English Literature, AP World History, Theatre, and French in Memphis-area high schools for forty years. Parker-Lawrence's essays/poems/fiction have appeared in *Slice of Life Magazine, The Barefoot Review, Stone Highway Review, The Literary Bohemian, Knee-Jerk Magazine, Prime Number Magazine, Tata Nacho, Orion Magazine, Wildflower Magazine, Memphis Magazine, Persephone Magazine, Edible Memphis, Southern Indiana Review, Unlikely Stories, Alimentum, The Ecotone Exchange, The Palimpsest Journal, The Commercial Appeal, World History Bulletin*, and *The Pinch*. Her nine plays have been produced in Tennessee, Illinois, New York, and Florida. She lives in midtown Memphis with her husband and two shelter dogs, Koba and Yashimaru, but she welcomes visits from her friends, daughter, five stepsons (three active in the US Army), and their families.

ADDITIONAL PRAISE:

"In *householes*, Natalie Parker-Lawrence, uses the hybrid haiku form, inspired by the haiku poems Richard Wright produced in the last year of his life, and characterized by rhythmic economy, precision, and surprise. The poems are conversational, snatches of things the women said about their disturbing experiences, selected, arranged, and performed with a spring or turn at the end. The result is the poems linger with authentic power and speak of lives worth knowing."

—Marcia Aldrich, author of *Companion to an Unknown Story*

"These poems are portals into the lives and harsh realities (the pills and whiskey and broken bodies) faced by female caregivers. The voices are raw and intimate, and made all the more real by flashes of startling tenderness. In this stunning debut collection, Natalie Parker-Lawrence's miracle is her ability to conjure entire worlds with a handful of words."

—Sonja Livingston, author of *Ghostbread* and *The Virgin of Prince Street*

"Deeply moving… often tender, painful, sometimes sassy and occasionally funny. Always raw and wise and honest. Some of it felt vaguely familiar. Much of it evoked sorrow and compassion for the lives represented to highlight the deeper challenges, emotions, of the Caregiver/Veteran experience. In many ways it felt very different from my own experiences. Ours, it appears, was a kinder, gentler journey. His PTSD manifested itself in quieter, more subtle ways. As did his dementia. There were definitely moments, increasing as he moved closer to crossing over, when he'd wake confused…still in a dream state…awaiting deployment orders from a Sergeant or some higher up. Often he'd see a young boy running thru a room (his younger self? I could only speculate). Because, the experiences captured felt, for the most part, darker, more painful than what I experienced with dad (with a couple of exceptions …ie, Ringo? … I wondered if the Vet had been a musician… loved that they'd called each other "Brother")."

—Chris Ciccarello, daughter and Caregiver of WWII Veteran

www.ingramcontent.com/pod-product-compliance
Lightning Source LLC
Chambersburg PA
CBHW031435150426
43191CB00006B/527